The Sheep of Celtic Herd
What Are Ewe thinking?

Roxanne Dean

Copyright © 2014 Roxanne Dean

All rights reserved.

ISBN 13: 978-1499716207
ISBN-10: 1-4997-1620-6

Dedication

I dedicate this book to my siblings for always being there for each other in times of need. Sheila, Lenore, George and Jennifer are a very important part of my life. Also, Bill my husband who has helped run our farm and has spent numerous hours putting in fences and taking care of the needed repairs and maintenance, along with humoring me for having many animals. I would like to thank my friend Kathleen Davidson for her expertise and advice on raising sheep. She has been and still is; a great help and inspiration over the years.

I also want to thank Demi for her time and help in getting this book together. Then of course, I have to thank my sheep for their individual personalities. Their stories and daily shenanigans have been my inspiration. Thanks to my daughter Bronwynn for helping with the editing as she is the real writer of the family! Finally, thanks to Rhianna, my creative daughter who has been able to convert the wool from my sheep to beautiful sweaters and rugs!

Acknowledgments

As a sheep owner for the last fourteen years, I have become fascinated by herd interaction and the similarities to people. The sheep have their own way of communicating to each other that is very basic but follows a pattern. Mothers have a special way they communicate with their lambs and the lambs do listen to them, sometimes better than kids listen to adults!

They also remind me of Elementary school kids. I spent my career as an Elementary School teacher in various grades and assignments. I found that I have to be able to figure out what they were up to, and how to keep ahead of them. It is the same with the sheep. Once they get to know you, you can work with them. The key is to do it in a positive way.

Anyway, the poems are a result of watching and learning. They represent the point of view of the sheep or my point of view of how the sheep respond to me. They are meant to be for fun and entertainment, just as the sheep have been a constant entertainment to me over the years. They are work and they are fun. Humor is necessary in order to consistently take care of them.

My photos of them have won ribbons at various photo contests including: Maryland Sheep and Wool, The York Fair, and the York County Camera Club. This year I had the opportunity to win the Best in Show {Blue Ribbon} in the color landscape category showing the snow scenes from this past winter. Several of the photos show the human expressions and the humor that they are capable of.

The back cover sheep illustration is a design by my creative sister "Sheila" who has been writing poems about family members for years. Her illustrations frequently add to her poems.

Thus, I asked her to come up with a design that went with the subtitle: What are Ewe Thinking?

My first Shetland ewe was named after her! Sheila, the Shetland ewe is my smartest and the alpha sheep of my herd. I have included some short stories about some of the ewes. We can learn from the sheep. They can remember people and things for years, and just like people, some are smarter than others!

TABLE OF CONTENTS

It's All About the Food 1

Herd Interaction..11

Social Interaction..17

Whatever the Weather 29

Celtic Herd Farm 39

Ode to Cold 45

Shearing Time 55

Snowy Winter...61

Fleeces and Pieces 73

Sheila the Sheep Thinking..80

It's All About the Food

It's time to eat again,
Oh, don't act so surprised.
A little bit of hay is good,
It helps revitalize!

This little mouthful that I grabbed
Is barely just a morsel.
It will help me get through the day,
Then I'll be more resourceful.

Snow

The snow is getting deeper
It is now above our feet
If we don't start heading back soon
We will not get anything to eat!
Our fleeces all look white now,
Our colors are all coated.
We slowly get into a line
And start following the leader.
We're sure that everyone soon will get
some food from in the feeders!

Celtic Herd

We are the sheep of Celtic Herd
Acting like humans is really absurd!
They make strange faces amusing to us
They give us treats and make a fuss.
They squeal and squeak, make bizarre faces
When we run around, having pasture races.
It doesn't take much to amuse the people
Just look real cute, act like their equal.
Is it worth it? After all, we are the rookies
Yes indeed it is, just give us cookies!

Cookies Please!

We beg for animal crackers.
They are a treat we really love.
We can eat them gladly all day
Long, if you let us,
We'll push, jump and shove.
The taste, they are delicious.
The crunch has a wonderful sound.
The shapes, they do not matter,
If some of them hit the ground.
We'll eat them from your fingers,
We'll eat them out of your hands,
We'll push on top of other sheep,
It doesn't matter how they land.
Just give us some more cookies,
Even if they have animal shapes,
Especially ones that look like tigers,
It is great that you don't have to bake.
Even little ones we'll devour,
Any shape or crumbs you have,
We'll lick our lips, stick out our tongues,
They're yummy and we're glad!
We'll even search your pockets,
We know you have a bunch.
We've found them several times before,
So it's more than just a hunch!
Oh no, you have no cookies.
We will stop and look forlorn.
It's your fault we just love them,
We've had them since we were born!

Attention

Rub my chin and scratch my ears,
I love attention when you come near.
My eyes will close; I'll stand real still,
I love attention and need my fill.
I push away the other ewes,
I get so comfy, the others lose.
My tail starts wagging like a dog,
I'm almost chirping like a frog
Don't go, I sigh, and you are gone.
I hope I don't have to wait too long!

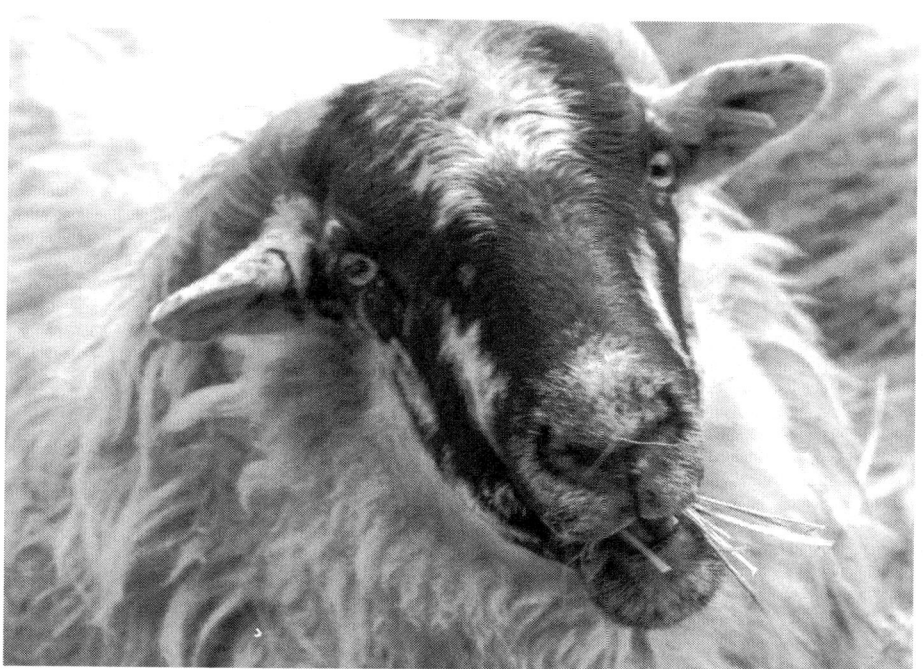

questions??

What do we have to eat today?
We are as hungry as we can be.
We recognize that bucket of grain,
And are waiting eagerly!

When are we going to eat today?
It seems we waited far too long,
Yesterday wasn't nearly as bad,
Hurry, and bring the hay along.

Where are we going to eat today?
Is it pasture one or pasture two?
The snow keeps blocking our path up the hill,
And we never know what to do!

Why are you taking so long today?
We are starving, can't you see?
Maybe you should bring some extra grain along;
We keep hoping that you do!

When are we going to eat today?
Yes, we actually asked that question?
Come on, you know we can always eat!
It's cold, we're sheep! You reckon'?

Watch the tongue!

Why do we stick our tongues out you ask?
We are hoping for a treat to make our day last.
Funny faces we make when we get something to eat,
It looks like we're smiling, so happy we bleat.

We wag our tails when we see you near,
We hope for a treat when the coast is clear.
We try hard to push and get up front,
It's the only way we can get what we want.

A nice little trick is to climb on another's back
This way our mouth is closer. It is a food attack!
This works quite well and a lot of us have tried it.
We stick out our tongues; we don't even try to hide it.

Chewing all day long is a habit that we savor.
All you have to do is feed us, the tongues explore the flavor!
Keep lots of vegetation handy and we won't need this favor!

Sheep Lines

The lines are getting bigger,
The sheep keep moving along,
More ruminants are joining
Their fleeces are nice and warm.

The weather is cantankerous
It is snowing very hard,
The wind is blowing loudly,
The sheep act like they're starved.

They see me coming with the bucket.
Their pace picks up a bunch
If I don't get their quickly,
I might become their lunch!

It's not that I don't feed them.
That I certainly do each day,
It's just that patience is not their virtue,
So I quickly throw more hay.

This only stops a few of them,
A pause, a chew, some time,
The line soon breaks, the race begins.
They run like it's a crime.

Herd Interaction

We are Scottish Blackface Sheep

We are a breed of Scottish Sheep
Not your typical "wee lassie."
We have big bones and a pretty face,
But we can be real sassy.
Our horns are part of the entire breed,
The rams and ewes both have them.
They give us character you might say.
Be careful though so they don't bend.
Our fleeces are white and very thick
To help you make your rugs.
They make a beautiful accessory
So warm, you will give it a hug.
If you are cold then grab a skin
And wrap it all around you.
The warmth it gives can't be surpassed
It will quickly spread throughout you.
Our faces have a unique shape
A black and white pattern of such.
We photograph extremely well
And you'll love these photos very much.
We are sturdy animals that can endure the weather.
It's part of our heritage, we make a nice, warm sweater.
Harris Tweed jackets come from our coarse wool.
Many patterns have been created and woven for a thrill.
So if you are ever traveling around anywhere in the UK,
You will find us everywhere, at some point in your day!

What Are Ewe thinking?

Do sheep have conversations with each other?
What would they really say…?

If one of them got mad, if another sheep ate their hay?
Would they comment, "Excuse me, you are taking up my space."

Would they laugh if ewe told a joke and baaa with a long snort?
Or have a ewesful pickup line when Rambo is a sport?

When discussing politics, or events out in the pasture,
Would they jump around and yell with loud bleating just like laughter?

Sometimes they have expressions, that look a lot like people,
But that is crazy! Don't you think it sounds like a soap box sequel?

twins

There are two of us, we look alike, not like the other ewes.
We stand the same, we are unique, and wear the same size shoes.
We're black and white all in our face, a special type of pattern.
We're Shetland sheep, we're fun to keep and no we're not from Saturn.

Our colors blend along our backs with nice, soft, crimpy fleeces.
You'll love to touch it oh so much, and twirl it in little pieces.
We have some grey and brown and tans with colors so unique.
They look quite well out in the sun along with our physique!

We have a hundred different markings that describe the Shetland Sheep.
So many, you will have a hard time to decide which ones to keep.
The two of us are such good friends, we don't like to leave each other,
When one of us gets lost or hurt. we'll just go and tell our mother!

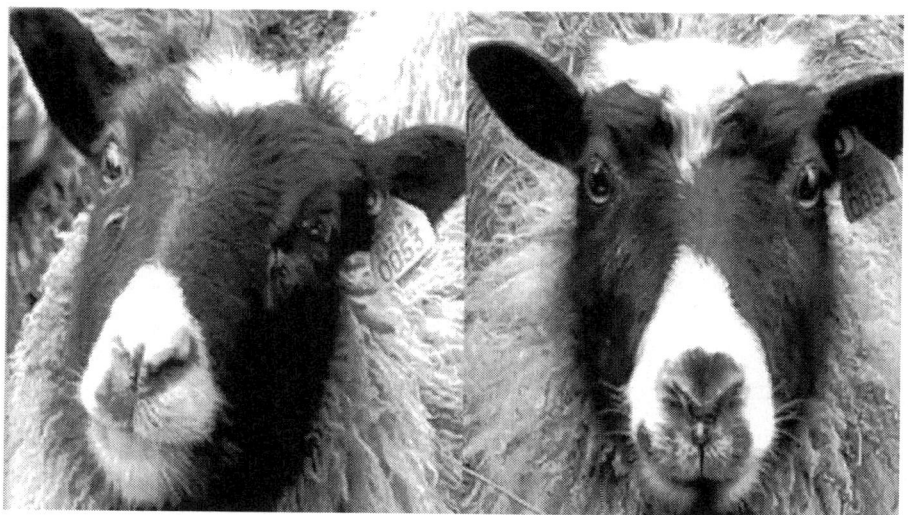

Social Interaction

What are they thinking when nature calls and they suddenly have a meeting?

Is there a pickup line? Or does the ram just wait for comments and a greeting?

Does she look at his horns to see how well they contour along his face?

Or checks him out to see if everything else is in the right place?

Do they go for colors or are they just blind, and waiting for some interaction

Or do facial markings help them decide if the looks add to the satisfaction!

I Herd About Ewe Two

I heard about you two sheep.
You are very sneaky, the word has leaked.
The problems you cause when you are together,
Makes you, annoying you're birds of a feather.

You manage to push the others away,
So you can stuff your face with all the hay.
When it's time to eat, you attempt to shove,
You aren't letting the others see any of your love.

The only reason we keep you around
Is your fleece, it's soft and warm like down.
You also are also cute and have a certain look
You're smart but just remember,
We are on to ewe; you're not off the hook
Since we can read you like a book!!!

It Wasn't Us, We're Innocent!

You can't blame us for all of this fuss.
We're herd animals and got caught up in the rush!
Just because you saw us strolling about,
Outside of the gate is where it's all at!

WE were munching in peace, and wandered around,
The fence ……… it just came open!
The wood was weak and falling apart
And the metal chain was broken.

We have some weight,
And leaned against the post until they bent,
Then suddenly we moved along,
And didn't know where we went.

The grass was green, it rolled along,
And where it went, we followed,
It sure was good, it lasted long.
We bit but never swallowed!

We're really upset you think that we did something
Really baaad… when it actually was nothing!
We hope you'll forget, don't give us that look.
Let us back in, don't plan on having mutton!

the view from the top

We sheep love to go up high
We'll go to the top of our hill.
WE can sit there for many hours
Ah the view- can't get our fill!

WE can see for miles all around us.
There is plenty of fresh air.
The neighboring farms have cattle close,
Whose voices that we share!

The grass will soon start growing
And the weather will begin to get warm.
A taste we love, we'll do the mowing,
And eat true to our form.

Sunny days are quite inviting.
Ah, the grass is green all day.
We will not need any extra at this time,
No supplements or hay!

We sit and chew, keep our heads down,
Keep an eye out to take in the view.
A predator might show up for a visit
Or something else to join our zoo!

If you ever hear a whistle sound,
It is meant to be a warning!
That silly dog that lives above,
He likes to visit, so we'll start forming.

We put the younger ones inside
As we start to get together.
Some of us are simply more mature,
Stay out and make things better.

Then when things start to settle,
We'll go back to being lazy.
This is the life we're meant to have-
Eat, sleep and chew – *not crazy!*

Double Ode to the Cold Or... Woe to Ice

This year has been eventful, it has barely even started. The snow and ice are awful. There is no place to cart it!

The snow keeps piling up, with lots of ice hidden underneath. I look funny when I'm walking as I pigeon toe my feet.

I keep looking at the ground since I don't want to end up falling. My gait is slow and deliberate like gears that just keep stalling.

So far it seems to work as I shuffle here and there. If I do fall it doesn't matter with all the clothes I wear!

It takes forever to get dressed so I can go outside. I am so well- padded with these garments that are warming up my hide.

It looks like I have put on weight as the layers keep piling on. Who needs a gym with times like these, the workouts keep you strong.

The ice can be destructive, with its own majestic nature. My rooftop looks like scenes out west when we went to visit glaciers.

My sheds are more like mountain tops about to avalanche. Just don't walk underneath the edge or else you risk a chance.

My pool has now become a frozen lake encased. You can't tell where the ground and cover separate their space.

My vehicles are somewhere underneath the snow and ice. We will find them in the spring when the weather has turned nice.

The chickens altogether are laying a single egg. With all the food they're getting, they still want more and beg.

I heard someone say the other day they have created a new ex-ercise.
It's putting on 20 lbs of clothes and feeding livestock, is that wise?

Sheep-er-cise is what she called it while you walk with a bucket of feed. Stumbling along in piles of snow in order to fill their needs.

By the time that I am finished, I am sweating and exhausted, Bringing lots of snow with me in the house just like a running faucet.

Then you pile up the clothes around the woodstove with a fire. Then you notice you can't get near it as the garments keep going higher.

Don't forget the boots and mittens, the hats, the scarves and gloves, The extra pair of socks and jackets, all the accessories you love.

It is still only mid-February and the weather isn't getting better. Accu-weather says tomorrow it will be mild, cold and wetter.

If it wasn't for the beauty and the quiet peaceful scenes I can capture with my camera – I would end up being mean!

Hey Ewe!

Hey ewe, you butted me.
You snuck ahead in the line.
You are not supposed to do that-
Yet you do it all the time.

You are certainly impatient,
You haven't got a clue!
Learn proper management single file,
Don't try to make it two!

I will really butt you next time,
If you try to block my view,
So get back to where you started,
Or this warning will come true!

You're pushy and annoying,
Your manners they are lacking.
If you keep pushing near me sheep,
Your butt, I will be smacking!

Okay that is much better, ewe,
You are getting the idea.
So I will get ahead right now,
Good-bye, Adios, I'll see ya!

We're Glad

We're glad that you think we're funny.
We're glad that you are amused.
We find it endearing that you enjoy us.
You would agree if you were in our shoes.
We're happy that you gave us cookies.
We're happy that you rub our chin.
We smile when you come near us,
We'll never be the least bit thin!

Who You Calling Fat?

I can't believe you have the nerve to tell me, I am fat.
I carry lots of muscle and that's all there is to that!
I am fluffy and good looking and I like to eat all day.
I work it off when strolling about and sometimes even play.
I have to keep up my energy you know,
It is something that I need to do.
I can't believe you are calling me names
When you say chubby, it isn't true!
When my fleece grows back in, you won't get to see all this muscle.
I don't hurry very often and I don't see any need to hustle.
You have really hurt my feelings, this time you have gone too far.
I am still your little lamb and the one who is the star.
I see you have some cookies for me, now that really is more like it.
I'll forgive you now since I won't need to remember
This and cookies help to keep me fit!

Ode to Wool

Wonderful, wispy, waterproof, wearable fleece.
The feel of the sheep that you left behind
Is still in your scent, an image in my mind.
Your scent either smells like hay or green shrubs.
The lanolin visible with black marks when rubbed.
Your texture is crimpy, it's springy it's soft.
We keep you protected and away from the moths.
Ah! The colors you bring, very pleasing to look at!
Grays, blacks and white and even milk chocolate.
The shades that are blended already with whites,
Their naturally colored that change in the lights.
You are very strong, your fiber we spin.
A craft project waiting for a scarf to begin.
You will end up as roving or maybe some yarn.
A warm pair of socks that someone will darn.
Shaped into a hat or even a sweater,
That keeps someone warm in the coldest of weather!

Whatever the Weather

Trinity, the Shetland Ewe

Trinity the Shetland ewe started moving around in circles as the raindrops started to land on her wooly fleece. Her light moorit shade was one of the unusual Shetland colors. She had a distinctive white face that went right down the middle and was bordered by the moorit color that she owned. This marking was not uncommon in Shetland Sheep. It was closer to a rust color. All in all, she was a very pretty looking ewe. She was also quite friendly and loved her animal cracker treats as did all the sheep in her herd. Her facial markings put her in the category of a Smirslet.

This was only one of the many color patterns that belonged to this particular breed of sheep. There were over sixty distinct patterns and markings. She also had two white socks on her back legs. Several of the ewes that were born around the same time as she was also had white socks. A few had only one white sock, some had two white socks and one of the ewes had three white socks.

This was a genetic characteristic that was passed on by the sire named Petey that was added to the farm several years ago. Petey moved to a new farm but his offspring still carried the white sock gene along with a white mane and varying grey colored fleeces. Some of the ewes were black or gray and black with a patch of white on top of their head. The white would fill in part of the face or along the eyes and would stand out with the sharp black color of the rest of the body.

The wet drops started falling softly at first so the sheep didn't mind. The soft drip, drip, plop, on their heavy wool fleeces was hardly noticed. After the cold winter, they had nice warm wool coats so this type of weather was not even an issue. The water was absorbed quickly into the thickness of the wool. Thus the sheep continued grazing on the tiny bits of green that had recently started to push through the soil.

The mixture of rain and sun kept the grass cycle going. Although now the soil was a good bit muddy and there really wasn't much green at all. They received a daily ration of hay to give them needed protein, and a grain mixture that was necessary to provide body heat.

Trinity and her group didn't need to drink that much water when the ground was wet. There was plenty of moisture available. The older ewes still liked to get their fill of water from the buckets of water that lined the pen. The people changed the water so it wasn't an ice block all the time.

When there was snow on the ground, the sheep ate the snow in large scoops. Their tongues would flick back and forth enjoying the light fluffy texture of the snow. Snow had a pleasing sensation and the sheep could get large scoops of it quickly and as often as they liked. There was no need to push in line to get at the water buckets when the snow was spread throughout the pasture.

Now the wet rain was starting to hit them harder. It now contained clumps of ice that would sting their faces and become a nuisance.

Sheila, one of the older ewes started to turn and head back into the pen. It wasn't long before some of the younger ones also started following the leader. Then a few more, and gradually most of the ewes started a line in single file. They casually walked along until most of them were now inside where they were out of the heavy rain.

Trinity looked for an open space in the barn over in the corner she stopped, and plopped down in the hay. The rain was now making zinging noises as it hit the metal gates. Sleet was now part of the wet mixture that the sheep didn't like. Eventually only one or two stragglers would still be standing out in the open. Depending on how thick their fleeces were, would determine whether they would realize the rest of the herd had gone. Baaing, they would start running to catch up. Passing the fences with clumps of wool along the bottoms, they would hurry to find an opening in the barn to squeeze in.

As the winter was started to wind down but still cool, there would be days that would be too warm for the sheep so they would find a section of fencing and rub their wool back and forth. It was also a good way to scratch their backs. Lots of small pieces of wool attached to the fences and wood posts, like flags blowing in the wind displaying many varieties of colors and thicknesses. Thus the term" wool gathering" was added to the old sayings. Kids were actually sent out to collect these scraps of wool at one time so that they would be added to the wool pile for spinning. Nothing was wasted. As much of the wool as possible would be gathered off of fences and gates. These bits of wool were already long and thin and ready to be spun. Lots of fiber could be collected this way along with larger clumps of wool that was rubbed off the fleeces. It was not unusual to see a sheep with strands of wool being dragged alongside them. A section of fleece could be pulled out; this was known as "rooing."

Wool is the best fiber for making mattresses and rugs, because it is naturally flame-resistant and durable. Wool clothing is good for humid and damp weather, because it tends to absorb moisture. Wool clothing pulls moisture away from the skin so people don't have to endure that uncomfortably, clammy sensation. This is also why sheep can stay outside during wet weather.

The barn would be crowded while the rain was coming down, splashing mud all over. The sheep that couldn't fit into the barn would sometimes be half in and half out and would get wet. The bigger ewes would push the little guys out of the way if they wanted in. Several of the sheep just plopped down in a corner to wait out the rain. Most of the time the rain didn't last long, and one of the leaders would head back out. Soon there was another row of sheep following them out into the pasture. If the wind was too strong, they would just stay where they were, or lay down flat on the ground to stay out of the wind.

There was always some hay to nibble on inside that got pulled and stretched to all corners of the pen. The younger sheep would get a head start to the hay .They also learned the technique of keeping low to the ground so they wouldn't get pushed aside.

Trinity learned how to slide between two or three bigger ewes and get underneath them to get at the feed. Others learned they could stand on the backs of the sheep in front of them causing them to slide over and then slip in and get a mouthful before the bigger ones came back. It was a constant shuffling for a good spot to get at the feed. Definitely an Olympic sport! Head butting was done constantly but only as needed. Not like a sports game with unnecessary roughness! Thus the smaller ewes remained small and the bigger ewes got bigger! Definitely survival of the fittest! However, many of the ewes in this herd looked pleasingly plump. They were all well fed.

When the feed bowls were empty, it was not unusual to see the lambs sprawled out in the bowls. These were comfortable to sit in while the lambs were still small. Twins would both climb in a bowl together and take naps like that. Sometimes only a back leg would stick out while the lambs would be cleaning up any remaining food inside. The feed containers were to the lambs like playpens were for humans. Except with the lambs, you could see legs sticking out or half in and half out of the bowls.

Kells, a black Shetland ewe with two white socks and a white section on her face, was one who enjoyed taking naps in the left over remains of a kids' turtle sandbox.

Feeding time each morning was like a three ring circus. A constant changing of sides and moving to different feed containers was all part of the ritual. It was amazing how six sheep could all fit their heads inside a small area that had feed in it. It was often comical to see only the rear ends of the animals, since the heads pretty much disappeared only to have one resurface covered with feed and struggling to catch a breath. It was like there was a bottomless abyss. You would think they would need to come up for air more often than they did. (This was the ultimate food fight.) If there was an eating contest it would be hard to declare a winner. Once in a while, one of them would come up for air or shake its head after almost choking from grabbing too much grain.

The sheep didn't mind the cold weather except when it was partnered with strong winds. Then they kept close to each other for added body warmth. On the other extreme, on very hot days, the sheep would scratch out a spot in the dirt and keep low to the ground to keep cool.

Snow was another story! If it was snowing hard as in a blizzard, the sheep would head for cover and then would not come out if the snow was too deep. Sadly this happened during a February a few years ago. One of the ewes decided it was time to lamb. There was not enough room in the barn since all the animals were huddled in the pen and the newborn lambs were suffocated almost as soon as they were born. It was a sad thing to experience.

Fiona, the mother seemed to be in shock and had lots of milk. Luckily she ended up helping nurse other lambs that were born out in the pasture a few weeks after this storm had passed. She didn't end up depressed like some moms could when they lost their babies.

If snow was at least a foot deep, sheep would not move around in it. They would wait for someone to flatten out the snow so they could walk in it. Sometimes, if it was too deep, it was necessary to get a snow blower and clear out a path. Then the sheep would walk along the path in a single file and turn around and go back. This constant back and forth in that path could keep going on for hours at a time. It was one way to get some exercise.

It was comical to watch, especially when the leader stopped and they all stopped as if on cue. When the leader moved again, they all moved along in the same fashion. This is where the term following like sheep came from. It is amazing how we use these terms to describe people too! The only way a new path was started was when one of them bumped into the sheep in front and then fell out of line. This would be the beginning of a new path, and thus the cycle would continue.

As the snow melted or got down to a size that was lower than the sheep, more paths were started. These areas that got worn down by constant traffic were still visible in the dirt when all the snow was gone. When driving along where the top of the hill made the pastures visibly, one could clearly see lots of paths crisscrossing the fields. The flock itself was usually close together while grazing.

After everyone got some feed, they either went to find some water or moved around seeing what was new and what they could get into. Curiosity was always a sport with nothing in particular in mind. New things were always out there to explore. Fences to were meant to be pushed against or at least get a good back rub. A row of wool would flap in the wind like small waving flags. Once again, one ewe would start to move, and another would follow, then another, till a whole line was walking in a different direction.

Finally, it would be time to take a nap. Mid-morning naps broke up the daily routine and allowed the sheep to be energized for a busy afternoon of chewing and munching whatever was available. A few of the sheep would play a butting game and flip and hop with hooves in the air. This didn't usually last long as one would get distracted and see something to eat. Food was the ultimate goal in life. If there was no grass available, the sheep would get animal crackers as a supplement a few times a week. They also loved to eat apple pieces and got the left -over's and cores when an apple pie was made.

Carrot pieces were also a favorite but the animal crackers were the best. Some of the sheep would almost do tricks to get this delight!

It wasn't unusual to see them jump on another sheep to get up higher and closer to the source.

Whatever the weather, there was always a special treat. Even when the trees were knocked down after a storm. These greens were not wasted but used to feed the sheep and they even peeled off the bark quickly. Then a pile of branches would be sorted into a heap so that they could be burned when the weather was decent enough to do so.

time to Move On

When do the sheep know it is time to move to another location?

Sometimes we know it is time for a change. We can't continue doing what we have been doing. We become stagnant in our ways and ideas.

Someone has to make the decision to change. Will it be a self-guided one? Or will it be a decision that was prompted by someone else? Maybe a look, an action, or just a comment has caused the initiative.

Regardless, a movement has been made, maybe from the momentum of several people. The move might be slow at first, as when one sheep turns around and starts to walk down a different path. The rest of the herd is quick to pick up on any movement and soon another sheep will follow, then another.

The ones that haven't followed yet will slowly look up and see the group moving. They will run to catch up, so they won't be left by themselves. Protection is important to them and the herd is always safer in a group. People have the same tendencies. They are resistant to changing on their own.

Someone has to take the initiative. There will always be a leader and there will always be followers.

You can always find people that have similar interests to your own if you look hard enough. The first step is to see what direction to take and there is a bit of uncertainty that goes along with this decision. The progress is slow at first but soon picks up either for better or for worse. As we see others moving along and trying new things, it sometimes gives us the boost we need to try something new.

Celtic Herd Farm

Snow, Mud, and Rain

Snow, mud and rain, oh what a pain,
The combination of such makes it very lame.
You slip and slide and then fall down,
How many times have you hit the ground?
You can't even walk, you pretty much slide,
You look like a creature that should go and hide!
You don't want to see what you look like now,
Just go inside and grab a nice warm towel.
Some days it is best not to go outdoors
If it wasn't for the animals we can't ignore.
The chores get done regardless of the weather,
A washing machine will make the clothes better.
Or maybe a car wash would be a better choice?
Don't scream or pout or use a loud voice.
When you are feeling clean and your spirits have lifted
Try going back out, since the weather has shifted!

Muddy Sheep, What a Hoot!

Muddy sheep what a hoot,
They are captured like my boots.
Mud is a creature that grabs and holds
It is splattering all over my boots.
The sheep try to run and are twisting about.
Their hooves are caked more like cement blocks.
I slip, they slide we can both barely move.
We are both trying to maneuver their daily food.
I don't want to go down; I try to stay clear,
But they push against me till the ground is near,
Oh what fun it is to stay in the ruts,
Try to keep standing or act like a klutz!
It's time to find the washing machine,
If I make it back and give up this scene!

Ram

What a handsome, delightful, creature you are!
You ruminant, you know that you are a star.
Your horns are unique, curled, not a flaw.
You're the boss of the herd, everything is your call.
You have the great look of self-satisfaction
We are in awe at your stylish fashion.
You should be on the cover of a magazine
A model you are, and you should be seen.
Your markings are striking, your colors sublime,
You should own a mirror to look all the time.
A perfection of nature, that's who you are.
Your lambs will be too, and they will go far.

Finnola ewe-lamb

Ewe are the spitting image of your dad,
He was good looking and so we are glad,
You have all his markings that are so unique
You are a moorit ewe with the classic white streak.
You have the white socks that give you style
The genetics that you have will endure awhile.
You are a classic lamb, you're almost his clone
You remind me of your sire wherever you roam!
He was Finn and you are Finnola
You both have colors that look like granola!

Ode to Cold

It is cold out today,
I don't want to go outside.
But I need to feed my animals.
I wish I had their hides.
The thermometer has a reading
Of only minus one,
It wouldn't be so bad,
If there was a lot more sun!

It is cold out today,
I put my carhartt's on.
I adjust the straps up to my neck,
And stretch the clamps, what fun!

I grab my heavy jacket.
I pull it over my head.
I am feeling warmer already,
But I would rather stay in bed.

The wind seems to have picked up
As I am venturing to the outside
Contributing to the chill
So it takes me for a ride.
It is cold out today.
But when I feed my animals,
The enthusiasm they portray,
Makes me happy they're not Cannibals!

Sheep jokes

Why do people use us for their jokes?
They really like to ramble...
Their material is pretty sheepish, it's more than they can handle!
When the relatives from Philadelphia come out to our farm to visit us,
They say EWES GUYS to our face and make a lot of fuss.
So when you come to visit, we hope it's with shear joy!
Since you are the ones that are comical and get to listen and enjoy.
We will entertain you with ewesful tricks that are really something!
Just don't leave us with that dreaded line
And tell us that we know mutton……..

Petey Ram

Reflections from the ram
I am who I am
I was meant to be.
A classic I was
…and my offspring are me!

Sheepskins of Every Color

What color is the prettiest of all the ewes you see?
I personally prefer the black ones, They look unique to me.
They show up in the pasture when all the sheep are running.
They stand out in the herd, when the others are out sunning.
Their eyes look like they're glowing in contrast to their fleece,
There aren't that many black ones; in fact they are the least.
They have a tint of brown, darker than the others.
Some have bits of white on top, not unlike their mothers.
They are the most unusual as far as combinations, especially
Their faces have markings with striations.
They are a type of Scottish Sheep originating on the Shetland Isles.
They have a lot of Viking names, their faces all showing different styles.
The markings have some colorful names with many variations
The mogets, krunets, fleckets, and lots of other odd creations.
The smirslets, mirkface and yuglet sheep should be the Maybelline models.
They have black rings around their eyes, in lots of shapes and styles.
The grays and whites with faces black, have such crimpy fleeces.
Some of them have a pinkish nose and tongues with very long reaches.
Regardless of the colors, the moorits, browns and blacks.
They stand out with such perfection, there is nothing that they lack!
Now that I have had this discussion about the colors,
I find I love them all, and will have to check out the others!

WHAT?

What are you looking at, you Shetland ram?
We see you watching us, you really are a ham!
You think you are clever and are causing a fuss.
You come into our pasture and start chasing us!

You simply can't decide who you like the best.
It's whoever pays attention to you; you're so like all the rest!
You are quite a handsome dude, we all do agree.
We soon become charming and stop trying to flee.

We can't be too picky there is only one of you.
So let's start a line and let you get through.
You snort and you holler, you simply can't decide,
So pick all of us and we'll stay at your side.

We'll become part of your herd and await your reaction.
Let's face it; this group is a source of satisfaction!

tongue in Cheek!

Tongues are mostly pink you know,
But some of them are black!
You can tell a lot about genetics
By looking at this app!
Some of us have tongues that are different.
We stick them out, real-ly!
The color that our fleece will be
Is easy to tell by the tongue you'll see!
If we have a darker tongue,
We're really quite unique.
Give us a cookie so you can peek
At what goes with this physique!

Back to Back

I got your back and you got mine.
This way I can eat all day and everything is fine.
If you see anything approaching us,
make sure that you yell and make a fuss!
This way we can all graze and ponder.
Not having to worry at all- what is there out yonder.
Soon it will be your turn to start the munching,
Try the grass on this side, it is great for crunching.
Then we'll move on, but we will still keep together.
This plan of action always seems to be for the better.
Both of us together are usually very wise.
We are able to keep watch with an extra set of eyes.

Crossbreed

I am a cross breed, a hybrid to be exact
I have characteristics of two different breeds
I am both Shetland and Scottish Blackface for a fact.
I am sturdy and strong, I am a survival of the fittest
I represent the sheep of Scotland inheriting genes to be the swiftest.
I am mostly white with splotches of black
I wear a pair of horns with pride and long fleece you can abstract.
I have legs that are white with black around the edges
I often have some spots of black that fit inside like wedges.
I am covered with long fleece from head to toe
I am nice and warm and a good blanket to stow.
I have a personality that is the best of dame and sire.
I will supply a lot of meat if that is what you desire.

shearing time

Shear joy

The weather is getting milder.
You can smell it in the air.
The birds have started chirping,
The atmosphere is fair.

The fences are being moved around,
That means we'll start changing pastures.
You'll makes us go through narrow lines
To get the food we're after.

We will follow single file,
That is what we are meant to do.
As soon as one of us gets started,
The rest of us will move.

We know that something is going to happen.
We're curious just the same.
Until we hear that buzzing sound,
We think it's just a game.

The sound is very scary,
We huddle and we freak.
We see that guy that makes that noise
And escape is what we seek!

We turn to run and find
The way we just came in is closed,
We're stuck. Oh No! What should we do?
This herd is tight, it grows!

So one by one, we get snatched up
And tossed so we're upside- down.
This feeling is just horrible
And our face is in the ground!

It's embarrassing to see your feet
Sticking way up in the air.
That buzzing thing attacking us
Sounds like it's in our ear!

Stuck In the Fence

I hate it when I cannot get
My head out of this fence.
I cannot move, my butt is stuck,
Can someone get a wrench?

You push and pull me like I'm dough
You are kneading into bread.
I know I've put on a few more pounds
And there's more to me to spread.

Just get me out of here real soon,
So I can get back to eating.
I soon might starve if left like this
And you will hear me bleating!

I only do this when I'm sheared
Without my wool I'm thinner.
As soon as it grows back again,
I'll join you all for dinner.

It's only my head that's stuck again,
The rest of me is fine.
The only problem is that I can't move
And some of me is behind!

A simple push to get me out
Would surely make me grateful.
Don't criticize or make fun of me,
I don't want to act real hateful.

I do this simply because I can,
There is no rhyme or reason.
It doesn't matter if it's hot or cold,
We're goofy any season.

I am a sheep, you can't predict
What I might try to do,
Just help me out, it'll work
If you'll just see me through!

SNOWY WINTER

It's Snowing Again

It's snowing again, will it ever finish?
We want to go out in the fields
And this stuff will not diminish!
We don't mind a few more inches
As long as we can get around.
But when it keeps on piling higher
Our short feet can't find the ground.
When it is up to our furry fleece
It is hard to move too far.
We need someone to push it out of the way
And to keep our fence ajar.
It starts to become annoying even though
We're not like people.
When we're stuck inside an area
We start to repeat a sequel.
It is even worse when icy,
Then our hooves begin to freeze.
The wind keeps right on howling
And it's more than just a breeze.
Can you get that tractor out here?
Please push us out of this rut,
Otherwise it gets too boring,
And we'll jump, and push and butt!
It is harder to find grass now
So we just will munch on the hay.
Chewing, chewing, and more chewing
Is pretty much what we do all day!

that Furry thing

That furry thing with the pink tongue
Likes to slobber on me, all over my nose.
He comes close to me and I don't mind.
He's only trying to be my friend, I suppose!

He runs a lot and doesn't stay still.
He follows us up and down the hill.
He needs a job that he can do.
It's watching us, keeping us in view.

He jumps around and makes funny sounds.
The rest of the group doesn't like him around.
He's my buddy now and we get along,
As long as he is on the side he belongs!

Who Do Ewe think is the Cutest?

If you had to pick out one of us
Which one would it be?
Which of us is cutest of this group of three?
Do you prefer the pink nose or the one with the best smile?
Take your time, don't hurry, you can answer in awhile!
Would you prefer the black and white face
That comes with the dark black nose?
Or would you choose the light moorit shade
With long crimpy fleece in rows?
Do you go for our expressions?
We know we're just so cute,
Why don't you give us your decision,
You act like you are mute!
Oh you can't make a decision,
you like us all the same.
We understand your hesitation,
and know you're not to blame!
We all have our qualities that enable you to like us,
Our markings are so unique you can't help but fuss!

Lambs

You little guys are amazing, you have a certain look,
You act like you already know it all. but you haven't read the book,
Your colors are always different with lots of combinations.
You can change within a week or two with splotches and striations.
Your eyes are very pretty, they flicker when mom is near.
Your little face is just too cute and your calls to mom are dear.
You can get loud when you are hungry or when you are upset.
You hop around and jump for fun but your legs are still not set.
Your energy doesn't last too long, you take a lot of naps
The way you move is really odd, it reminds us of a rap!
You play a lot with other sheep who are close to the same size.
The bigger ones will call the shots since they act like they're wise.
You are very entertaining and make us laugh at your transactions.
You keep close to mom and that is good, she watches all your actions!
You are a furry ball of wool and smell like the newborn that you are
You have already touched our hearts, you are a shining star!

Line Leader

Who gets to be first in line,
It can't be ewe, you were the last time!
You always forget to give someone else a turn,
If you don't let me move up now I will act very stern.
You are acting pushy you know. I won't be your friend.
You need to get out right now and go back to the end.
I will not move an inch, I will plant my hooves firmly.
If you don't move along soon, My mood will be sternly.
Why don't you reconsider, you are starting to give in,
I can tell you were teasing me, it is obvious by your grin.
I will keep right on going till I get to the front.
It is what I always strived for and exactly what I want.
Oh, it is great to be the leader of the herd for a change,
Even though there is no one in front of me
And that sure is strange!

Best Side

Make sure you get my best side when you take my picture.
It makes a difference when you do and it will come out richer.

I need some time to comb my fleece and get out all the tangles.
It looks much better on the side when you get all my angles.

Make sure you have your camera ready and get my point of view.
It is amazing how good I look with the right lighting, I'm brand new!

Be sure to focus all your shots and let me pose a little bit.
Don't get too close or I'll be blurred and start to raise a fit!

Herd Patterns

We wander up and down the pasture
To see what we can find
We move together in a herd
With foraging on our mind.

We can keep a line diagonally
Or one that is horizontal
We are like a landscape painting
That really shows our style.

When you look again in an hour or so
We are nowhere to be found.
We can move so fast that you are scared
That we are not around.

Don't worry we'll show up again
After we have had our nap.
We put our heads down on the ground
And make ourselves look flat.

You might not see us right away
When you first attempt a glance.
We have a tendency to blend in
With the grass and disappear by chance.

Then suddenly you will see
Some heads bobbing up and down.
With lots of green stuff on our heads
That make us look like clowns.

It's great to have a lot to eat
And mow right through this brush.
It makes our bellies nice and fat
So that we don't need that mush.

When you see a few of us
That means the others are not too far.
We stay together in our herd
And that isn't too bizarre!

Seeing Double?

The ewes have lambed
and everywhere you can see,
double ewes, more double ewes,
not simply X,Y,Z.
It's a b'ewe'tiful sight!
Little baaashful ruminants everywhere!
Idolizing their mothers
with soulful eyes to stare!

Maaaa

Maaa, I adore ewe, you are amazing,
I stare at you so long my eyes are glazing.
When I am hungry you are always there
How can I help but sit
    and   stare……

Skinny For Awhile

Look at me I am very thin, all you see of me is skin.
I was just sheared the other day, and now I have no fleece in my way.
I can move around without getting delayed.
That fleece of mine kept getting frayed.
It was way too long and slowed me down
I got in caught in things, it made me frown.
This way I feel that I am free, I can run a lot faster, this is the real me.
My true colors show my pattern of gray
It is striking to see and is here to stay.
If you like to knit and need a gray sweater, come back next year after the winter's cold weather.
My fleece will be back and I will look much fatter.
The crimpy feel will return with the colors that smatter.
My face will remain the way that it is now.
Don't confuse me with that strange Jersey cow.
I still look pretty and my patterns unique.
My muscles are flexed, what a great physique!
So tell me I am gorgeous, I don't hear it enough
I will smile for your camera and continue to look buff!

Fleeces And Pieces

Are You My Mother?

What happened to my mother?
She used to be that skin.
They took all of her wool from her
And now it's a box she's in!

She still smells like my mother.
I recognize the scent.
I keep on baaing and calling her
But I don't know where she went!

My mother is just sitting,
She's nothing but a lump.
She seems to be stuck inside that box.
She's huddled in a hump.

OH Mother, why aren't you talking?
I can't even find your smile.
You continue acting like a lump
And I know that's not your style!

Wait! mother, I hear you calling.
Yet your sound is over there.
How did you get out of that box
Without anything to wear?

Now this really is confusing.
You have taken on a new look.
The rest of you that's in the box
Was how you used to look!

Well, anyway I am happy.
You still smell like yourself.
I am overjoyed that you came back
And got to keep your health!

Buddies

We sheep have buddies just like people,
We sometimes hang out in twos.
When one of us decides to move
The other one follows on cue.

We use each other for footstools,
If we need to reach something high.
We can balance on the back of our buddy
There is no reason to ask why.

We tolerate unusual behavior
If one of us tries out something new,
We don't questions or ask another,
Not any weirder than what people do.

So if you see a sheep acting weird
Remember that is our normal.
We like to be spontaneous
And we're not trying to be formal.

So if you start to laugh at us,
Remember, we're different but for real!
We think that you are the strange ones
The way you talk and squeal.

We tolerate your funny sounds
And the pictures you take of us.
We don't mind it when you give us treats
And make a lot of fuss.

This is our type of zumba class,
We don't need to find a gym.
We exercise our jaws a lot
And don't worry about looking thin!

Can Ewe Spin A Yarn?

Can ewe spin a yarn?
I'm sure that you do,
You are always talking
About the stuff that we do!

Our yarn is for spinning,
It starts out as a fleece.
Then it's processed as roving,
A big ball in one piece.

It is great to make something,
What else can we say.
It is pretty to look at,
Especially the gray!

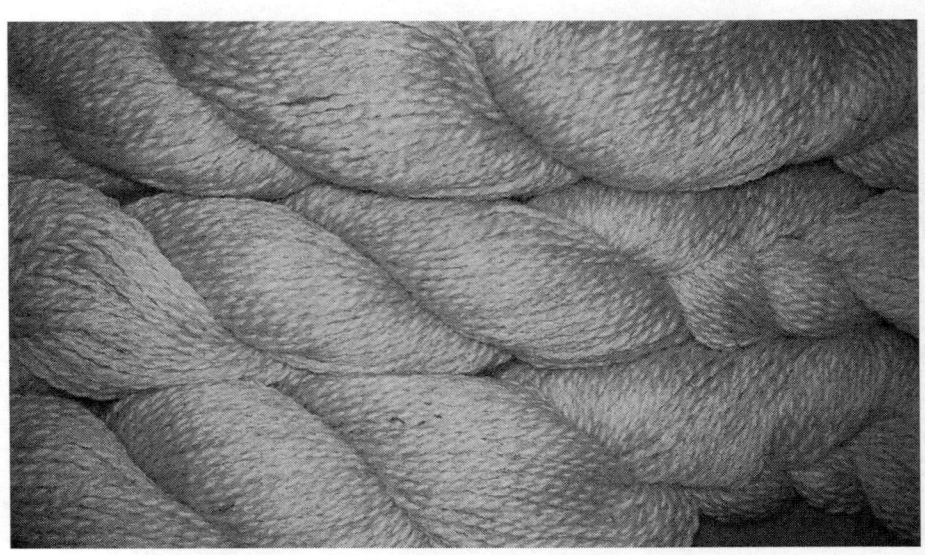

Sheila the Sheep thinking!

Sheila is a Shetland Sheep
That looks like she is thinking.
She stares at you and has a look
That seems like things are clinking.

She is the alpha ewe
And shows that she is very smart.
She is quick to see when things are changed
And leads with all her heart.

She loves her lambs and takes such care
To make sure that they are near.
She doesn't let them get too far
And makes sure the coast is clear.

If she spots a predator
She will give a long loud whistle.
The herd will then begin to form
Like they were shot right from a pistol.

She then will move away
From all the noise and the commotion.
She keeps her distance from the crowd
Like the caboose on a locomotion.

She loves for you to rub her chin
And then paws you like a dog.
She wants her cookies and her feed
And can act just like a hog.

Sheila is a special ewe
That acts like she is thinking.
When she lets you rub her chin
It seems like she is winking!

About the Author

Roxanne Dean lives on a farm in Glen Rock, Pennsylvania. Her farm is Celtic Herd Farm where she currently raises Scottish Sheep and rare breed chickens. She loves to take pictures of her Sheep enjoying their daily lives. Roxanne is a retired technology teacher from Baltimore County Public Schools.

Best of Show Maryland Sheep and Wool 2014

Made in the USA
Middletown, DE
15 May 2016